Articles

This month's cover:

Coloring design
drawn by
feature artist
Kendall Bohn;
colored by
Jane Adam.

Tangitude Publications

Founder, Coloring Wizard
Extraordinaire & Editing Ninja
Mary J. Winters-Meyer

Marketing Marshal
Anisa A. Claire

Super Cool Brainstorming Ninja
Stephanie Anders

Artists

Kendall Bohn from Kaleidoscopia
Augusta Schinchirimini
Dwyanna Stoltzfus
Ellen Million
Jeanette Wummel
Laura Anne Passarello
Luciana Guerra
Mary J. Winters-Meyer
Valerie, Harry & the Fisch
Valpyra Skullstyr

Authors

Jason Hamilton
Mary J. Winter-Meyer
Shelly Durham

Color On! Magazine is a digital magazine founded by Mary J. Winters-Meyer and Shyla Jannusch, published monthly by Tangitude Publications, P.O. Box 17623, Urbana, IL 61803-7623. For subscription information, visit our website at http://ColorOnMag.com.

All rights reserved except where expressly waived.

To make changes to your account online, go to ColorOnMag.com

ISBN: 0692710833
ISBN-13: 978-0692710838

I0115827

Scribbles from the Sketchbook

AHHHH! MAY IS here! It is a month of bright flowers, new growth on trees, grass turning green, and baby animals and birds. No wonder the U.S. decided to celebrate Mother's Day in May!

Are you enjoying the warmer weather? Are you pining to get out of your office now that the days are longer? Does your desire to color get set aside for a bit while you head out to your garden to create colorful living landscapes?

We can understand that. It's a great time to enjoy the outdoors! But even in the nicest months there are windy days or thunderstorms that keep us inside. It's always good to have your coloring designs for those days when you just want to watch the rain hit the window from your comfortable recliner or couch.

This month, we are graced with a number of fun designs from Kaleidoscopia owner Kendall Bohn, a tutorial about coloring on fabric, and another installment in Jason Hamilton's skin tone tutorials. And of course, we've brought you designs from some great contributing artists as well!

Remember, we always welcome your feedback, and feel free to send any of your burning coloring questions to CrackedCrayon@ColorOnMag.com.

The Color On! Team

A chat with Kaleidoscopia founder and artist Kendall Bohn

By Mary J. Winters-Meyer

ARTIST KENDALL BOHN has been creating coloring books since 2002, and also publishes other coloring book artists under the Kaleidoscopia imprint. His designs, and those of the other artists he publishes, are wonderfully fun to color. Read on to learn a little about him and his art.

Color On!: What made you decide to start publishing coloring books under the Kaleidoscopia name?

Kendall: Some friends and I were having coffee, at Mill City Coffee Shop back in 2002; I showed them my drawings and asked if anyone had an idea for a title. We brainstormed for a few minutes – came up with lots of words. Someone said kaleidoscopic – that didn't fit; the next was cornucopia, and then someone said "Kaleidoscopia."

That was it... The title for my first self-published coloring book was *Kaleidoscopia a Creative Coloring Adventure*. Then with my next book in I decided it worked better as my business name – *A Kaleidoscopia Coloring Book ABSTRACT ADVENTURE*. Now I have the business name "KALEIDOSCOPIA" trademarked.

Color On!: Your books have an interesting twist with the "cloned" designs. Tell us how you came up with the idea of doing this.

Kendall: My business partner, August Johnston, had the idea while scanning and editing my drawings. He was working on the *MASHUP ADVENTURE* designs. We printed a few out and showed them to a bunch of people to see the reaction. Many actually liked the clones better than my originals, so we decided to add the clones along with the originals.

Color On!: There are a huge number of Kaleidoscopia books out there – how do you decide what artists to publish?

I like to see, unique creative ideas, and the quality of the line work is important to me. After I've accepted an artist, I send out the contract and then it is up to the artist if they want to be part of Kaleidoscopia.

Color On!: How do you create your art for your coloring books? Tell us about your process for creating new work.

The original abstract drawings in my books are hand drawn, ink on paper. I've also combined hand drawn with digital, and created images digitally. Depending on the subject matter, I might make stencils if I want to repeat a specific shape. After the drawing is finished, I scan the drawings then edit and do touchups to them.

Color On!: Do you create other art besides designs for coloring books?

Yes... I do oil and acrylic paintings, sculptures, photography, ceramic and drawings for my coloring books. My paintings cover a range of size and subjects from outer space to undersea with everything in between. My sculptures are created from many mediums as well. I've created marble, sandstone, ceramic, metal, and wire sculptures. I have a three-year long project photographing the construction of a bridge, that has turned into a few paintings, a sculpture, and soon I will be making a coffee table book with the best photos.

Color On!: Do you enjoy relaxing with coloring books by other artists? If so, do you have a favorite artist or book?

I've colored many and had lots of fun coloring the images of the artists I am working with. I've colored most of the Kaleidoscopia covers. I've had lots of fun coloring Lonneke Holla's *Crazy Creature Collection*, Lizzy Blu's *Lighthearted Lunacy*, Loni Gansmann's *Tangled Angles*, Racheal Mayo's *Dragon Adventure* and Ann Marie Irvine's *Ann's Doodles*.

Color On!: What color or colors do you most love to work with?

I really like working with all colors. It is about harmony and balance. I've done monochromatic paintings using blues or purple or green or whichever color I want or feel at the time to create the desired image. I've painted sunsets with the entire spectrum, and abstract paintings with as many colors as I could come up with.

Color On!: Tell us a little bit about your art. Do you have a favorite piece that you created?

Every piece of art has some story. I don't think I really have a favorite piece of art. I have a love/hate relationship with some of my work. Some pieces have more meaning then others. I am very passionate about all of my work. I have been very fortunate to have had the opportunity to create many different things.

Color On!: Other than creating art, what interesting hobbies or activities do you enjoy?

If I am not creating, I like to hang out with my girlfriend; she is very active and keeps me busy. Right now I have a part time remodeling construction job.

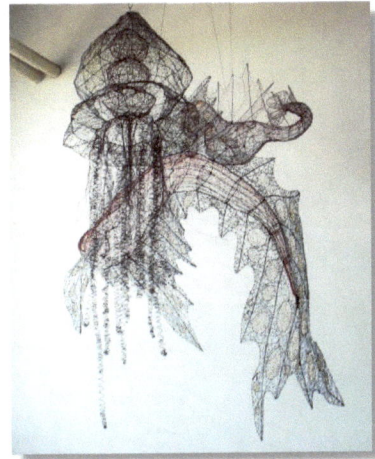

Color On!: Have you had any memorable responses to your art work from collectors?

During a coffee shop book signing a woman told me she is a recovering alcoholic. She said that she colored my designs to keep her mind off drinking. Another lady thanked me, and said how much she liked my abstract drawings. She told me that during her six hour, three times a week chemo therapy treatment, she and her daughter colored my books.

Color On!: If you had to choose one superpower, what would it be?

I would like to fly!

Color On!: Who is your favorite artist or artists (not necessarily coloring book artists)?

I study the painters Van Gogh, Monet, Renoir, Matisse and Vlaminck. My favorite sculptors that I study are Isamu Noguchi, Henry Moore and David Smith. Maybe most influential to my art are Wayne Tollefson and Cathryn Mulligan, my painting and sculpture professors.

While working I think about how to use colors to create light, define shapes, depth and time. I was influenced by the impressionists' use of color, and brush stroke. I also studied the fauvists for their emotional use of colors, shapes, bold brush stroke and the surrealists, for going beyond reality.

Color On!: Is there some person, place or thing that inspires you when you are creating your art?

Yes..... It all depends on the situation and what I am working on. Inspiration happens from all things. My girlfriend Tatyana, a colorful sunset, an emotion, an event, fireworks, losing someone, finding something in a dumpster that will make a perfect something else. This is where inspiration happens – creating something from nothing.

Color On!: Tell us about your plans for the rest of 2016. Do you have anything interesting coming up that you'd like to share with your fans?

I have some new drawings that will go into my next abstract adventure. Kaleidoscopia will be working with a few new artists who will be producing coloring books. I will be working on my paintings and sculptures along the way.

Color On!: Sounds great Kendall! We look forward to seeing great new coloring books from Kaleidoscopia!

Behind all your stories is always your mother's story. Hers is where yours begins.

Mitch Albom, "For One More Day"

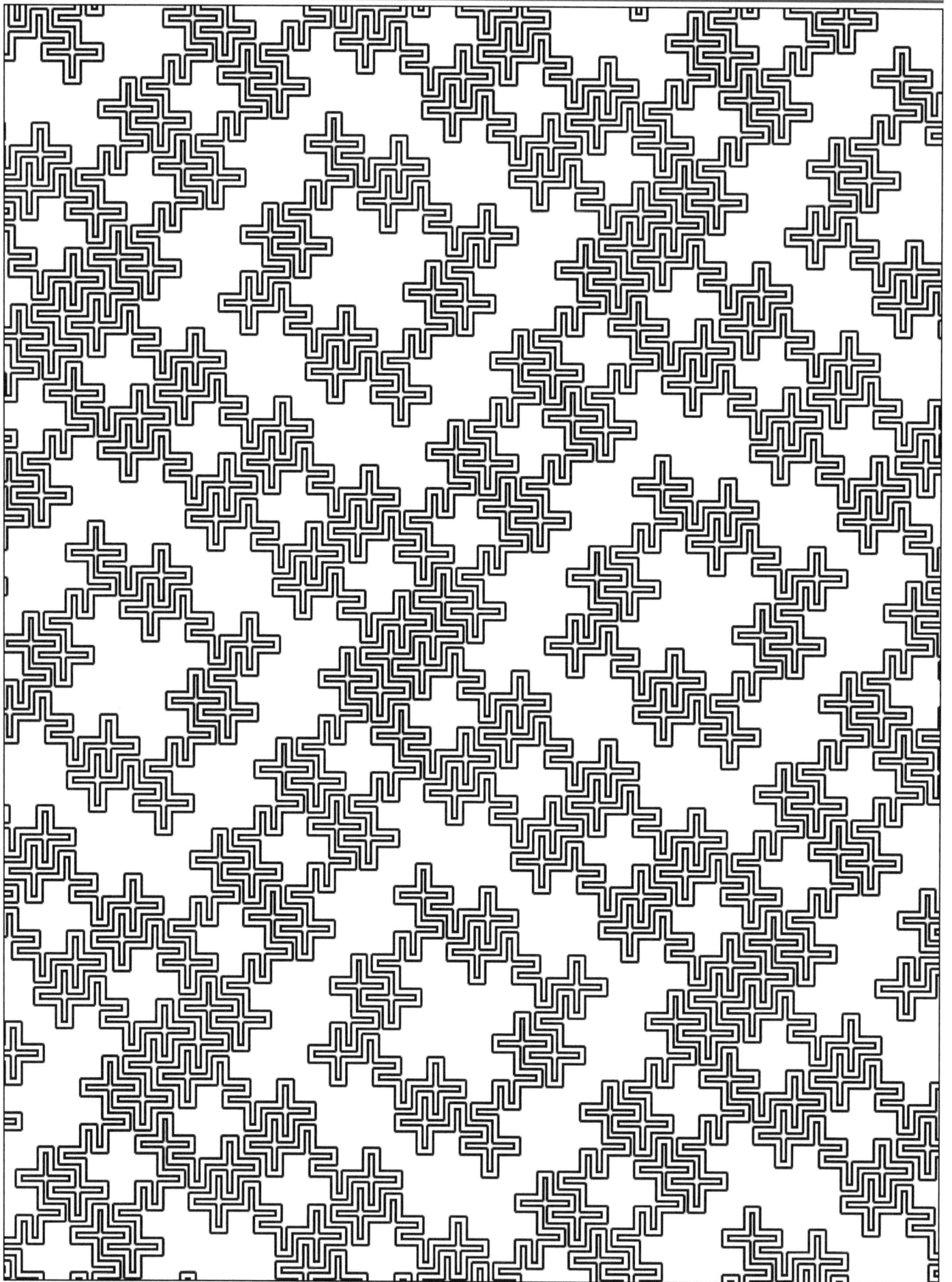

Coloring 101: Coloring on Fabric

By Anisa A. Claire

RECENTLY, I ORDERED a colorable bag with an Absur'D pattern on it. I was really excited to get it in the mail, couldn't wait, in fact, to get going on it. Until it arrived... then, suddenly, I became intimidated by the project and worried I would mess it up, costing myself money I didn't want to lose.

Sharpie and Chameleon

So, on went the research. I pulled out my Google-Fu and got to work. There were a lot of different options, but one name kept popping up... *Sharpie*. Well, just so happens I

love me some Sharpie markers and happened to have a small army of them. The one thing people were saying was that they ran a bit if they weren't 'set' first. Some examples showed a bit of runnage (is that a word? It is now!) after washing. Unfortunately, I didn't have what I needed to 'set' Sharpie so I just went for it and decided to spot wash my bag, rather than fully wash it in a washing machine if needed.

Sharpies work well, but there are a few things I noticed...

1. They bleed past the black lines fairly easily. I found if I applied less pressure closer to the black edges, it helped.

Close-up of Sharpie

2. They're time consuming, as they don't just 'flow' like some markers. You definitely need patience for Sharpies on fabric.

3. I had read that if you outlined the black with aloe, it would reduce the bleed. This is true, but it takes even longer to outline it all in aloe, and though it works, it's not 100% foolproof.

My conclusion for Sharpies is that if you're not extremely picky about little bits of bleed through, they are a good option. If some bleed through is going to bother you, I would not recommend plain Sharpie markers for fabric coloring.

The next on my list was Sharpie, again, but these ones are called: *Stained by Sharpie*. They are meant for fabric coloring. I snatched up a package and hit the bag again. First thing I'll say? Wow! What a difference from the regular Sharpies. They are easy to use on fabric, flow nicely and provide a full looking color. I was impressed, but these are the main things I noticed about them...

1. The color selection is extremely limited. You only get eight markers.

2. Of those eight markers, at least three are neon. I like neon, personally, but it has its place and I wouldn't want to be forced to color all fabric in neon colors.

3. Most of the pens did not bleed past the black line. However, the blue marker did. I don't know if it was just

Stained by Sharpie close-

this package or if all of the blue Stained markers are like that. This color, in specific, was difficult to manage.

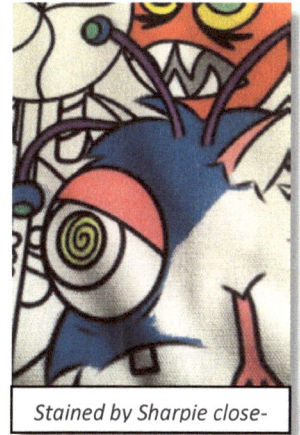

All-in-all, I liked Stained by Sharpie more than I liked regular Sharpies. My main complaint is that there aren't enough colors to really justify doing a full bag or shirt with them. They would be good for smaller pictures printed on fabric, such as team shirts or things of that

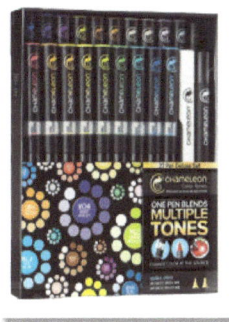

nature.

The next marker I tried was *Chameleon*. Now, I loooooove Chameleon markers. They're a bit pricey, but totally worth the extra money you have to spend on them. That said, I wouldn't recommend them for fabric. They're neat because they allow you to do shading on the fabric, but they run a lot and are quite difficult to control. So you end up with a lot of bleed through past the black lines. I only did a few small sections with Chameleon before I immediately knew that

*Close-up of
Sharpie (purple)
and Chameleon (orange)*

they weren't going to work for what I wanted on the fabric. Not to mention, they are a bit pricey, so it's hard to justify using them on a project that needs a decent amount of ink.

Finally, and very randomly, I stumbled across *Derwent Inktense* colored PENCILS. Yes, you read that right. I couldn't believe it, either. Colored pencils... for fabric? Can't be true. But yes, it is true! You can actually use Inktense colored pencils on fabric and they're *fantastic*. They are watercolor pencils, and there is a bit of trick to applying them. Here's what I did...

1. The color won't set if you don't wet the color. So, you can color it on like you would with regular pencils, and then you need a paint brush or q-tip to apply the water.

2. I didn't have a paintbrush, so I used a q-tip. It worked. You do need to dab the excess water off, though, or you will get bleed through past the black lines.

3. When you first apply the pencil, it looks lame. Don't get discouraged because once you wet it, it looks awesome.

Close-up of Inktense. Top is after applying water, bottom is just the pencil.

4. You can also dip the pencil tip directly into water and do it that way. You still need to dab off the excess, though. I found doing it directly in water actually gave me more control.

5. As a final step, you need to use some kind of Textile Medium to set the color.

Close-up of Inktense showing bleed with too much water.

Of the four products I tested, I would, without question, recommend Derwent Inktense pencils over all of the other markers I tried. If price is an issue, I would then recommend Sharpies, but urge you to remember... patience, patience, patience! They do work and the end result is quite nice, but you need to be extremely aware of your borders and the amount of pressure you apply while coloring.

I hope this article helps you in some small way if you're deciding to color fabric at some point. Grab a scrap piece of material to test and practice technique on first; that will save you a lot of heartache in the long run. Remember, though, that you CAN do it! It's totally possible to color on fabric and have it look nice.

Close-up of Inktense

Editor's Note: Remember that how much any marker bleeds is also a function of the surface it is drawn on. Different types of fabric will react differently than the cotton canvas used in this article. It's always best for you to test, either on a similar fabric swatch, or on an inconspicuous area of the actual fabric, before deciding what to use when coloring the item.

COLOR 4 FUN
COLORING BOOKS

Color 4 Fun was created in mid-2015 with a mission to publish books for colorists of all skill levels. Many of our books are designed specifically for those non-expert colorists who are intimidated by the overly-intricate illustrations found in the best-selling books. To our delight, "Seniors & Beginners" has been our most popular book.

And, Color 4 Fun has been a trailblazer with its all-in-one greeting cards and coloring books. Why buy two items when one will suffice?

Please visit our website at color4funllc.com to learn more about all 14 of our books currently available.

@2016 Valerie, Harry & the Fisch

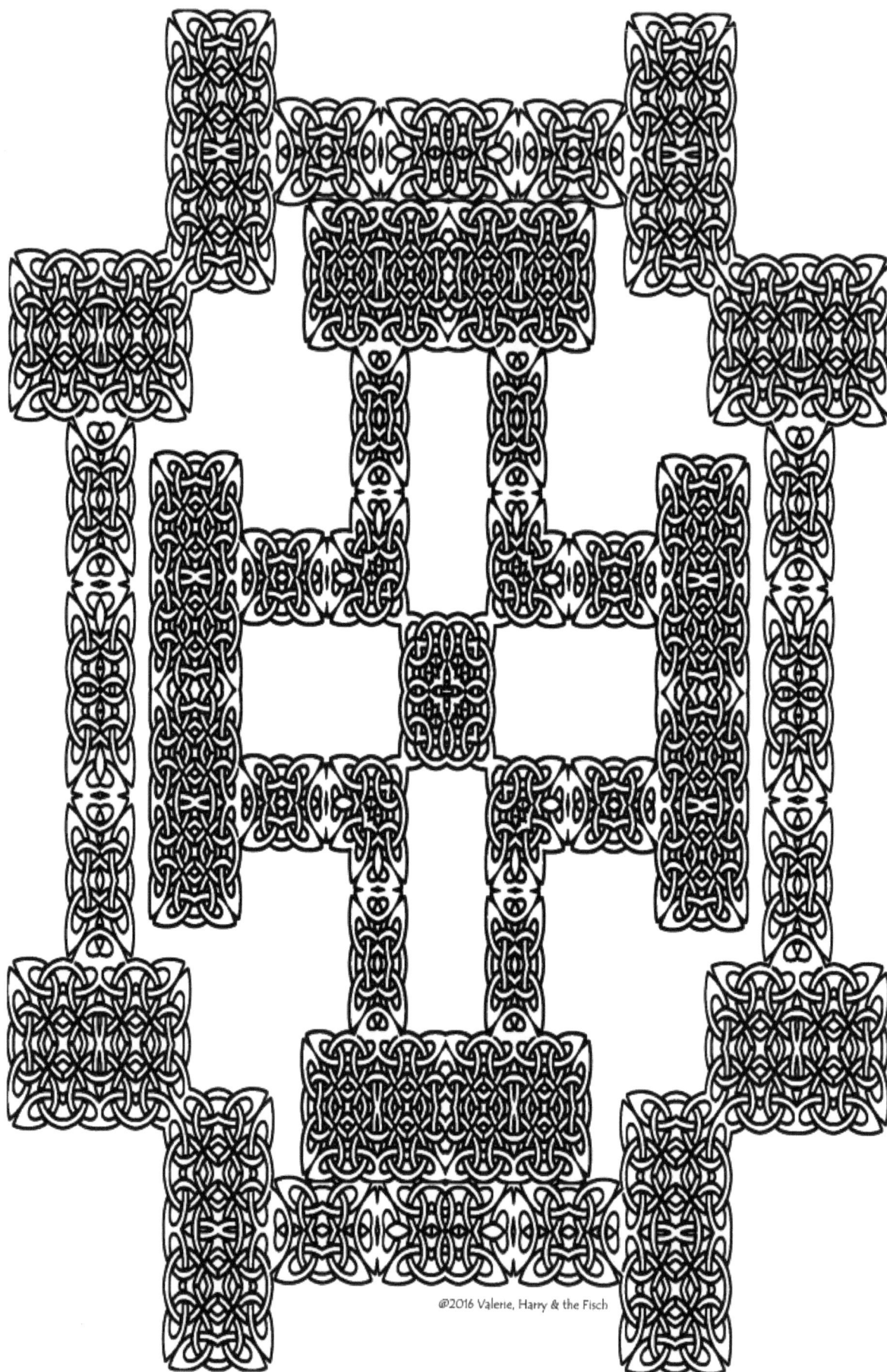

@2016 Valerie, Harry & the Fisch

Coloring 201: Coloring Fair Skin

Jason Hamilton

COLORING SKIN IS challenging, because skin is not one single color. We're not just talking about the various skin tones seen across the human race, but the landscape of every individual is full of highlights and shadows and reflected colors. Coloring in a person is not like

coloring a still life. We move, and so do the colors that play upon our skin. There's nothing wrong with cartoon colors. You can certainly pick up one pencil and color all exposed skin that one flat color. But if you want a more realistic look, then you need to move away from "skin tones" and select from a full spectrum of colors.

For our fair skin tutorial, I'm using the Italian woman from my book, *Color Me Beautiful, Women of the World*.

If you'd like to follow along with this tutorial, these are the Prismacolor colored pencils that I used:

- Sienna Brown PC945
- Mahogany Red PC1029
- Dark Umber PC947
- Beige PC997
- Mineral Orange PC1033
- Chocolate PC1082
- Ultramarine PC902
- Sky Blue Light PC1086
- Cream PC914
- Chestnut PC1081
- Nectar PC1092
- Green Ocre PC1091

I also used these colored pencils:

- Rose Art Cerise
- Crayola White
- Crayola Golden Yellow
- Inktense Poppy Red (not shown)

Picture 1: I lightly colored the face and lips with Nectar, which is very close to a flesh color. I applied the color more heavily around the eyes, sides of the face,

bluecatgallery.com

and shadows on the neck. I didn't bring the color all the way to the line on the left side of the face, in order to show a bit of reflected light.

Picture 2 (right): I added a light layer of Cream to tone down the red in her skin.

bluecatgallery.com

bluecatgallery.com

Picture 3 (left): I used Mahogany Red to deepen all areas of shadow and start working blush into her cheeks, nose, and hairline.

Picture 4 (below): This is the scary part because this stage never looks right. I start layering the browns to show more contour. The upper lip, eye socket, chin, around and under the nose and cheeks are building color and shadow.

bluecatgallery.com

Picture 5 (below, left): I evened the skin tone by using Beige as a blender

bluecatgallery.com

bluecatgallery.com

stick. This smooths over both the dark and light areas. I used just a touch of white to highlight over the lip, tip of the nose, the bone over her eye, and around her eye, and blended that with Beige.

Picture 6 (above, right): Scary time again. Deepen your shadows with dark browns and greens. Because everything else in the picture is white, this will make the face look unnaturally dark.

bluecatgallery.com

Picture 7 (left):
Color her eyes. I used blue, light brown, and pink on the whites of her eyes, and brown and yellow on the iris. Her lips got a touch of Mineral Orange blended with Beige.

Picture 8 (below):
I went over her hair with Dark Umber. I used long strokes going into the shiny areas, and then deepened the color in the shadow areas.

Picture 9 (below):
Hair is never just one color, unless it's by Clairol. Hair is thousands of little, well, hairs... that each varies just a bit in depth and tone of color and shadows and highlights. So, I added Chocolate and Sienna Brown to her hair.

bluecatgallery.com

bluecatgallery.com

Finally, I colored her headdress (Inktense Poppy Red) her dress (Prisma Ultramarine) and added Sky Blue Light and a medium cool grey for her blouse and sleeves, as well as the jewelry and background colors.

On final inspection her hair was lackluster so I went over it with Sienna Brown to add red highlights. You can't see it here, but I really like to add fine lines of metallic gold gel pen to hair, and to the iris of eyes to make them sparkle. I used a touch of RoseArt Cerise on her lips and her cheeks to bring them out a bit more as well.

...and that's it!

If you are interested in trying your hand coloring, visit my gallery page to download and print a free sample.

BlueCatGallery.com

the write your own story coloring book

valerie, harry & the fisch
ColorYourStory.com
ColorYourStory@gmail.com

Absur'D
Just Coloring Book for Adults
Candy Coated Kaos

J.A. Early Riser & T.J. Crayons

ellenmillion.com

©2016 VALPYRA

Color On! Oh! Color On!

JOIN THE FUN!
in the....

ColoUring for WEIRDOS

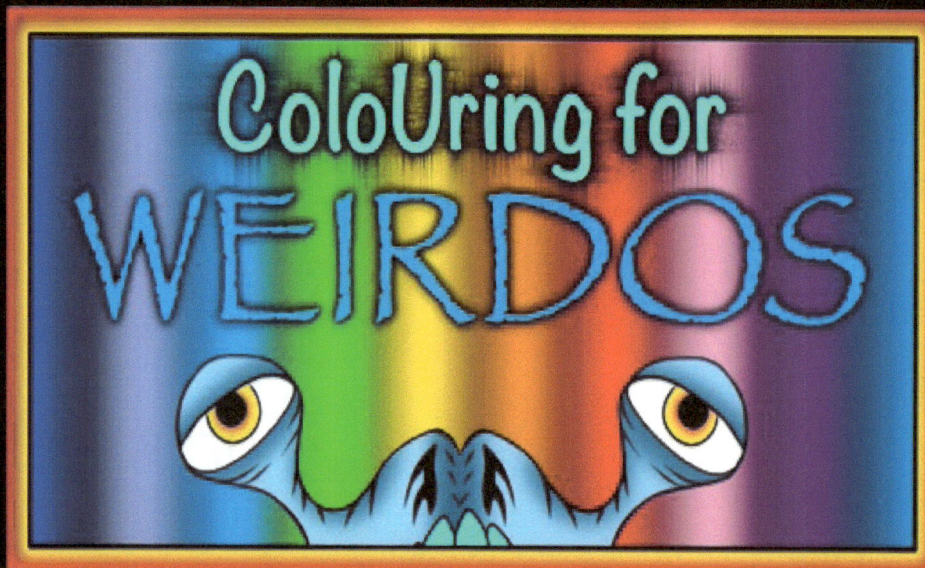

FACEBOOK Group!

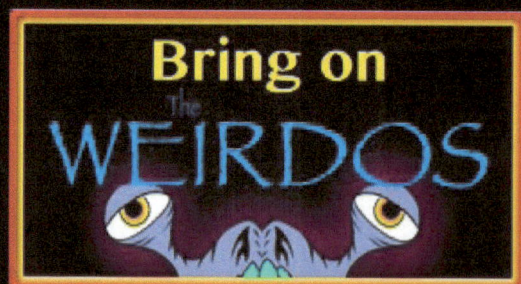

EMBRACE YOUR INNER WEIRDO

Bring on The WEIRDOS

- WIN PRIZES
- Try fun Weekly Weirdo challenges
- Share your coloUred pictures!
- Unite with your fellow Weirdos
- HAVE A BLAST!
- Browse other cool (and weird) coloring books
- Find FREE coloUring pages!   JOIN TODAY!